Blessings of the Beasts

¤

JANE SIMPSON

FUTURECYCLE PRESS
www.futurecycle.org

Cover image of marble columns (public domain); author photo by Michael Schwarz; cover and interior book design by Diane Kistner; Adobe Garamond text and titling

Copyright © 2018 Jane Simpson
All Rights Reserved

Published by FutureCycle Press
Athens, Georgia, USA

ISBN 978-1-942371-70-0

*To the people in this book—those named
and those not named*

Contents

Watching a Solar Eclipse.. 7
The Age of Discontent... 8
Daisy Bonner Wrote on the Wall... 9
Geese in November.. 10
Inauguration Eve, 1976.. 11
Metered Moments... 12
The People Wrote.. 13
Trying to Get It Right before It Goes Wrong....................................14
The Boehm Birds in the West Wing..16
Elvis Died.. 17
In the Absence of More.. 18
Those Who Work with Fervor at Three A.M................................... 19
The Shah of Iran Visits Washington.. 20
The Ra-Shalom Asteroid...21
Solar Panels on the White House.. 22
Papal Blessings... 23
Women in White... 24
An American Hostage Smuggles a Message through the Mail...........25
When the West Coast Heard First... 26
War Games.. 27
The Welterweight Challenge, 1980... 28
The Proletariat Breakfast.. 29
View from the Top of a Human Pyramid on a Moving Train...........30
The Dangers of Assuming an Outcome Because You Want It...........32
The Day After Losing a Re-Election Campaign............................... 33
Ways to Say Goodbye... 34
A Woman Who Knew What to Say.. 35
The Outlaw at the Omni.. 36
When a Couple Came Late to a Wedding....................................... 38
All of Them Mattered.. 39
Later Became the Time that Stayed... 40
The Family Eyes... 42
Simple Gifts... 43

Watching a Solar Eclipse

A total solar eclipse forced
the sun and moon into analytics,
into a celestial Venn diagram—
the heavens' logic, order.
Then, it was a wary watch.
Now, I see what I never saw.

The look back's still awkward.
And the words of time past
are problematic—things stripped
of edges and angles tend to bounce.
I worked for a good man.
He was the President.

But it happened and on the day
eclipsed I stood with That Good Man,
huddled in a small group—another
day at the office but on a roof
where the July heat baked tar smells
and the wind whipped us against doors.

The Good Man turned to me.
Write me a poem about today,
he said, as if I could write about shades
of light, night, and steely blue stressors
of the firmaments, as if I could take
ink and paper. Filter so many orbits.

The Age of Discontent

The woman who asked for a volunteer
in the campaign office wanted
a body, anybody.
She was tense, one who coiled tight
into the cord of her telephone,
who needed a typist to tap letter-perfect
for a man who didn't accept smudges.
I said, *Try me for a day.*
I typed with the telling points
of the left and right index fingers,
filled first a trash can with paper
I ripped from the roller
with purpose and ping.
I wasn't fluent in qwerty,
that coded language of the skilled,
and when the garbage was full,
I stuffed my purse with unuttered
damn-its and other arguments
of eye, finger, mouth, then took
my bag to the Ladies and emptied it.
Within hours I was spent,
a tattered flag in night dust.
I told her she needed a typist
who could look up,
smile and key within margin bells,
hit the space bar with disregard.
The woman was terse, resigned:
Work tomorrow.
If you like it, you can have a job.
She spoke with a cadence of sorrow,
a low voice of one who helps the inept.
She sighed words I imprinted—
faint, raised letters on typewriter ribbon.

Daisy Bonner Wrote on the Wall

> Daisy Bonner cooked the first meal and the last in this cottage
> for President Roosevelt. —April 1945

She was held down under the weight of stone
nested in weeds by dawn of Labor Day,
1976, when a caravan of buses left
Atlanta, went south to Warm Springs, Georgia
towards her kitchen in the rural hill
country that Roosevelt favored for the natural
order of farm, water, forest.

Miss Bonner would never have prophesied such
invasion: crowds to kick off the presidential
campaign of the local.
He was paces from the ivy, shingles, windows
that opened up a kitchen where her birthright—
name, place and purpose—
was covered in the yellow of old plexiglass.

This was an able woman who haggled butchers
over the marbling in beef, stewed rain-soft
tomatoes, sliced the early cucumbers
that still smelled of warm water, hot earth.
A woman who knew of timing—how the red juice
of roast would run into the tender of potato, the exact
moment rolls were brown and dusty as the day.

She left her bio scrawled in grief and bacon grease.
She would have warmed to a candidate who vowed
to connect, nodded when he pledged
to *give government back to the people.*
A woman who knew that sometimes a person
could rise up like the particles of light
and flour she'd sifted into the ceiling cracks.

Geese in November

Consider a campaign staff's migratory qualities—
geese in November—to understand the people
perched in a short-lease rental in D.C.
A room for clothes and eight-tracks,
except for John, an older man from Manhattan.
He'd leave on Fridays, fly home,
then on Sunday's he'd land at National,
hail a taxi, go home again.
He became storied the night he hopped from cab
to the curb, climbed eight steps to the porch,
wandered in and joined others on the sofa.
He'd entered the wrong house.
Sat for a moment with a family not his own.
He was a man who didn't worry about a furnace
flame or dead watts in a ceiling.
He never slid photos under the bureau glass.
Still, there he was, with the rest of us,
at work to mend the fences, put in solar panels,
a fellow tenant farmer—moved by the work.

Inauguration Eve, 1976

The day before, the waiters at Sans Souci
were ready for us:
Would you like grits with your chicken?
A city was grinding corn to line the bellies
of Southerners coming to town—workers
who'd sharpen pencils in buildings old as war.
Corn for those who would wear green passes
to climb cantilevered staircases.
Corn for those who would pile their laundry,
sour their milk unopened in refrigerators.

The day before, the street vendors were ready—
peanuts: boiled, salted, roasted.
Peanuts on scarves, key rings, all with toothy
smiles, lanky legs, top hats.
For the children, puppets without irony—
plastic legumes in tangles of limbs and strings.
The day before, the city brought back
agriculture to a one-company town
where merchants smiled at our drawls
with thin lips that covered their teeth.

Metered Moments

He played Chopin, Schumann,
Rachmaninoff, Bizet,
and, of course, John Stafford Smith;
only the wide ties and hair curls
of the audience cast the decaled
edge of history to a day in 1978.
I saw it on PBS. Cameras captured
Horowitz when he poured a Polonaise
in A-Flat Major, Opus 53, through airwaves
into the passages between floorboards,
hairline cracks at window casings,
split cuticles of early winter hands.

PBS didn't carry the Correspondence
Staff party at the Director's house
the first Christmas I was away from home.
We ate chili, played games on the rug,
clumped politely, awkwardly
at the piano for carols until Dr. Cook
of the Office of Personal Letters
poured a Piano Sonata #14 down
pores, ducts, electrical sockets, drains—
past want, into our seams and creases—
to nourish the loose soil around those
of us without the roots of home.

The People Wrote

Let me hear from you, he would say
to a town hall, and every day I watched trucks
bring hemp-hued canvas bags cinched with rope.
I saw mail-room workers deal letters like cards
into Post Office banana-boats, stack them
with the tooth-edged stamps up, to the right.
He'd get 100,000 in a quiet week, and they'd say
burn less fossil fuel, or more. Drill or don't drill.
Don't sign the Panama Canal treaty, or do.

I thought since they first went to him in small,
dark-curtained booths, the people found it easy
to confess; wondered if they wrote
because their husbands spent too many hours
in the oil-gray of the garage tuning an engine.
Because children picked the onion rings off bean
casseroles and called fathers for rent money.
Because on a long haul they totaled the fact
they wouldn't ever pay off the house note.

Thousands wrote after that malaise speech.
But Carter never said that word—*malaise*—
still the papers titled it and people
who wrote said he spoke to them, for them:
they of pen, pencil, Smith Corona told
how they lived with an absence of confidence,
and they knew he understood.
That's when it became a matter of beliefs—
his faith, their faiths, their faith in him.

So they wrote and we tried to answer.
The best we could do were replies on printed
cards, form letters that said thanks for writing,
typed letters from the President or, sometimes,
that linear Carter print in the margin of an original.
They wanted so much of him: a picture to stick
with a bank magnet to the refrigerator—
this was a man who carried his own garment bags.
They thought he, too, stood at the sink, eased a dull
steak knife into an envelope to open his own mail.

Trying to Get It Right before It Goes Wrong

I was summoned. My weekly sample
of mail to the President with the responses
typed and attached had raised questions:
Why do the replies have five carbon pages?
Carter wanted to know. My boss was irate.
Six of us gathered to track, count, account,
sweat over the tissue-fine fibers
of democracy, ponder the file system
of the Free World, prepare a treatise
on the pastel policy of saving words and trees.

Another day I went to the printers
where I watched *Time* magazines
roll off the press, waited for the run
of White House children's books
with the First Family, that cat, the tree house
in full color for children across the country.
The skin tones inked out caught-red, pink-shame,
thousands of sunburns, red necks, hands, ankles.
We can't accept these, I said, paling
the printer who threw the switch on the press.

Once an ambassador misspoke, in the easy
way words slip off a tongue and bounce
through long and empty corridors,
in the random way words take life
and grow into full-tongued mouths.
The President's office called. He wanted
to see the people's mail, hear the voice
of their words about the ambassador.
Carter sent the letters to the diplomat,
added: *This is what the people are saying.*

I didn't know much. I'd just learned
how to sharpen a nail
to pry under layers, strain my ears to hear
what wasn't said. I had to not say.

What was good was also a worry—
minute by moment I scripted, pre-scripted
the story thread for the consequence.
Once, I sent a report that said Chili, not Chile.
So first, I brain-typed it all, bold sans serif,
before it became a headline.

The Boehm Birds in the West Wing

In the Carter White House,
in the West Wing lobby,
the Boehm Birds roosted near
the door. They were sentries
with history, porcelain that came
from a patch of ancient earth,
formed by fire, by people
who stood at the sink and bathed
one hand with the other in Lava soap.

People who made those birds scrubbed
the way a man did who had hands
tanned into gloves in 6,000 BC.
The laborer of Yarim Tepe tasted
kiln ash that dusted the roads
of Mesopotamia, north of Mosul,
in that part of town where workers
lived—men without eyelashes
who fed ovens that seared their days.

The people who made those birds worked
the way a Cabbagetown mill worker
bent and rose, people from Atlanta
streets that boiled with the smell
of dinner. Laborers who breathed air
that floated with a soft white doom—
brown lung, Monday fever—where
a body sucks in toxic tolerance
and ague eases by quitting time Friday.

And then, there, the birds perched
in a cherrywood cabinet—a flock
shaped by men whose soiled fingers
became the wings that flapped ash
into live coals in a kiln so hot
it dried sweat before it dripped.
The Boehm Birds were the watchmen,
fixed in place by the hands
that made them, to be seen and heard.

Elvis Died

and a nation rang its president.
At mid-afternoon the first call came
from a beauty shop where the mechanics
of glamor—dye and dryer—
didn't squelch the moans and shrieks.
Calls came from a dress shop and a bank,
from braided wall phones in avocado kitchens
and in whispers from pink-tiled bathrooms
with starched linen finger towels.
Thousands of sobbing women, some men—
they were the angry ones who needed proof.
The switchboard swooned like a teen-age girl
and operators sent the calls to the Comments Office
since we had a nation in crisis.
I grabbed staff who could talk and, for hours
into the night, we took calls from heartland to coast,
receivers at both ears, two mouthpieces
positioned and timed for one message:
Thank you for calling. I share your sorrow.
But I didn't really. I didn't know
why they dialed their president,
went to a man they'd never met—for comfort.
Now, I know we spoke for a man they knew
would get their grief, *understand* the wails
from jailhouse rock and Heartbreak Hotel.

In the Absence of More

Louise, who loved her democrats,
dropped all, sped to the White House
when the Women's Clubs were asked
to volunteer—address the President
and First Lady's Christmas cards.

A woman of belly-fat age, she wore
sensible shoes, swirled cursive on four
by six envelopes. She took homesick
aides to her kitchen table in Bethesda
to share pie and her Bob's bad jokes.

Louise, who put the coffee pot on, stirred
cream and stories of how she stopped
sleeping when Adlai (of first name only),
lost, couldn't read the paper when Ike
ran the country, lost weight with Nixon.

Louise of the Easter dinner, the German
chocolate cake recipe she willed as her
legacy. Louise of the laugh when her
student sprayed Pam on a wire baking
rack and greased her linoleum floor.

Louise searched for truths in Plato's noble
lie, *That soup is not too salty,*
and she knew the upshot of trickle-down
economics but found nurture
in the dryer and navel lint of home.

It was only months after Reagan took office
that Louise wouldn't answer her doorbell,
hid her brain, its tumor, behind curtains.
She wanted to grieve alone. She never knew
I saw her pluck the apples I left on the stoop.

Those Who Work with Fervor at Three A.M.

No sleepers were asleep in their beds.
Not me—I worked late
in the night on the top floor
of the Executive Office Building.

No sleepers were asleep in their beds.
Not the mice that stirred the dust
that drifted from the second floor balcony
of the Indian Treaty Room.

Not the mosaic ceiling stars in that room
caught in the cataract-gaze of things old.
Not the light that fluttered like laundry
against marble floors, floating staircases.

No ghosts were asleep in their sheets,
not the specter that opened the locked
oak door, slammed it with disdain,
hovered between me and clarity.

No sleepers must nap at their desks,
not the guard who checked corridors
that echoed the thuds of his brogans,
the stammer of his two-way.

I saw his eyes settle, read his report
on the stretch of his jaw.
I heard the rail, saw the quick
who wanted to go home.

No workers should know the history
of dark in those halls at the hours
when the only blanket is the gloom
that settles between scalp and eyelid.

No workers who hear the furnace
inhale, exhale to the rhythm of their
own tense lungs should labor alone
to find relief in the creep of dawn.

The Shah of Iran Visits Washington

I look not to the things that are seen—
a hard edge to the South Lawn's blade and green.
The brass sheen, the glint of military band shoes.
The attendees come to a White House Welcome
where the band plays the National Anthem,
then the visitors' anthem, and respect
is softened by the clap of gloved hands.
Dignitaries are statues in a pose.
A visiting head of state stares—solemn-faced
and rigid as sworn oath.
It's a November day, warm enough,
but a slight breeze in the sun forces a squint.

I look to the things unseen, heard—
the protest chants off from the lawn,
the screech of police whistles,
sirens—those wailing women of the rocks
that beckon all to come and witness.
I feel that slight breeze, which takes
the tear gas from the conflict, turns it
and carries it across the lawn into the eyes
of all of us who wait for the address, the salutes,
into our eyes that well at the burn of currents,
into our aggrieved throats that choke on the drift
of stones crushed into fine desert sands.

The Ra-Shalom Asteroid

Drive down those country roads in Georgia
and you're bound to see how someone's
moved the cola-stained den sofa to the yard
to sit, shoulders wide and arms spread
across the cushioned back, one wrist cocked
for a wave and a nod to the sheriff
on his way to get his meat and three.

Workers moved a mahogany desk and
straight-backed wooden chairs to the White House
lawn, and it looked like Sunday afternoon at home.
Then Sadat and Begin joined Carter
on the grass, flags swagged, and the three men
stood behind the lawn furniture,
penned a page of truce for Egypt and Israel.

The Nobel committee gave prizes, and someone
named an asteroid after the Camp David Accords.
That's fitting—a heavenly body
to mark a lofty peace.
Scientists say the asteroid has an unusually
high surface thermal inertia,
a state of rest in an elevated air of heat.

That's the problem with peace. It's up *there*.
Only a few see it's at the end of outstretched arms
in the weeds and grit on grassless roads.
Only a few notice how children nap—they
drool and sweat, leave mouth rings on sofas
in their states of rest with higher body temps—
on home fronts of Cordele, Taba, Mitzpe Ramon.

Solar Panels on the White House

They were first installed in 1979, though
Reagan would rip them out only months later.
The Gipper believed, said, *Corporate
self-interest would steer the country.*
I thought Carter saw the energy crisis
as a holy problem—all those deadly sins,
all those personal weaknesses.
We said in mail about the energy war,
*You and I must do a better job of listening
to each other, acting with each other.*
I wanted then to get to the teachers,
the truckers, the executives, say
those panels let in heat and light,
those panels connect sun to core.
But we met a people who wanted to dig,
look deep for what they thought would
make it easier to get up and make coffee.
This was more than a three-hour wait for gas.
If we didn't do something, we would unearth
fossils, litter the kennel with sacred bones.
Still, his proposal's there, yellowed in place,
archived and buried under what came next:
more want, water bottles, big cars.

Papal Blessings

Should I wear a hat when blessed by the pope?
Girls in the Baptist church had to only worry
about covered knees when they sat in pews
on Sundays, when lost in the drift and drone
of words mixed with dust that floats
from the balcony, lit by unstained windows.
They knew well a yank of their hems between
mother thumb and index knuckle—patella piety.

What is proper for here-comes-everybody?
Does the Church have veil protocol? Should I
wear gloves? Is it against the law of Rome
for a Pope to touch female hands? Do I step away,
never turn my back to this head of nation?
Must a soul kneel deep in the mystery, light
small candles that make day into sundown—
rites Mrs. Byars skipped in Sunday School?

For the day, I dressed in modesty, hid knees,
buttoned high, no hat and fingers ungloved.
I sidled the receiving line, offered a right hand
while the Pope placed his left across his chest.
There's silence in the absence of color— palm
on a white porcelain cross atop papal fanon,
zucchetto on hair turned by age, the man
white-on-white of Tatra Mountains in winter.

And that blessing? It covered the pink skin
on my bare head. It exposed my face,
the way I bit the corner of my lip with my teeth.
The blessing put light on my knuckles uncovered—
my fists looked like they were kneeling
when I dropped them curled at my sides;
they became cups when I folded in,
melded the flesh of my palms and fingers.

Women in White

I wasn't sure why the women wore
white to march in 1920 for their vote,
but we, too, put on white shirts, skirts
when we paraded down Pennsylvania
to amend the Constitution: Equal
Rights, a law for equal pay that'd change
how dinner got cooked, beds got made.

Maybe it was homage to the matronly
women of the vote in 1917 in gloves
and silk-flowered hats. They could tell
a pound of apples by the heft.
They were women who carried banners,
circled stores in laced boots, chanted
with breaths cinched corset-tight.

White clothes worked well for the guards
who jailed the ladies for obstructing
the sidewalk traffic—blood runs redder
and women pale into their bonnets and bones,
turn ugly when they're framed by iron bars
and coiffed with kicks, sticks and fists.

Then come the fifties, and we were born
to fathers who said teach or type,
which was okay if I had wanted that,
but it was their crow,
their strut in the barnyard sun.
So we wore white when we didn't hunt
and peck—biddies that scrabbled dirt.

And July 1978, in Washington,
100,000 of us took to the streets.
We moved slowly, as if we had nowhere
to go—a bleached and beached tide.
We failed, of course; instead, we went
back to our jobs in our everyday clothes,
dress that wouldn't show soil and sweat.

An American Hostage Smuggles a Message through the Mail

His letter went by plane to 1600 Pennsylvania
where Lillie Bell was grim when she handed
the envelope to me, when all of us who touched
the thin skin of bad news huddled
with security agents to ensure
it was the fingerprint of an American hostage.

There were fingerprints from an Iranian mailman
who'd tossed the note from a letterbox into his sack,
took no interest in the serene-blue tissue-paper
#10 envelope with *United States of America*
printed upper left, in official business font.
Under that, *American Embassy, Tehran, Iran.*

There were my swirls, next to those from a hostage,
a man bewildered, like me, with his words.
A man who, like me, worked for his government.
He was from down the road—Falls Church—
told his family he'd see them at Christmas
and flew to Iran for a few weeks to sort visas.

He wrote December 26 to tell of days in the haunt
of darkness, night in the glare of incendiaries.
The words were plain, direct—fear
an invisible but indelible ink—the way his plans
to be home, to clean the ashes from his fireplace
were thwarted by his hands bound day, night.

Even now his message works into my skin.
I saw only the signature, the imprint of *it's just me*:
a man who wanted to drag the sticky stump
of a withered fir from his den; who wanted to ignore
the prick of dead needles on his wrists and fingers.
Check his mail for Christmas notes that arrived late.

When the West Coast Heard First

Helicopters crashed in the desert, eight men
died, and fifty-two Americans were not rescued
commando style——a military moment routed
by a trinity of wind, sand, and rotor blades.
The east coast had settled for the night so the west
heard first. Military wives watched CBS,
heard what, not who, and they dialed each other:
Do you know? No one will tell me anything.
Then slowly, gathering speed—a nation thought:
Call the White House, call the Commander in Chief.
Night and news rolled out—they jammed lines.

My call came at two in the morning—
Report to work, open the Comments Office.
There are no holds on night fear, no check
on emotion not lit and warmed by sun,
and those calls roiled through the dark, without
the tea-table kindness of volunteers to take them.
There were so many calls—I woke coworkers,
bosses who had people who answered their phones—
It was a rescue aborted, I need help.
Ours were voices in sweatshirts, stubble, bad breath
hunched in a small room littered with coffee cups.

We were the grim people of the wailing phones,
and I learned what people dread—
the unknown—listened to them demand to know.
I picked up phones by rote, said what I could,
but I knew we didn't have answers
for the army wife whose first child was due,
for the boy who worried about another draft,
for the steel worker who wanted the next mission.
I didn't know how to say, *Just wait, most of you
will see your loves again, you'll forget your terror,
find ease and light in what you know.*

War Games

Athletes lined the South Lawn in slouches—
in that way the fit look even stronger at rest—
but they wore faces bitter and grim.
They came to signify, honor their role
in foreign matters—Carter's boycott
of the 1980 Olympics, his decision
to use games to leverage the Soviets,
to protest invasion in Afghanistan.
None moved like they were the ice salt on frozen
war, like they carried the weight of body bags,
were a blockade on the thin lips of struggle.
The Olympians stood stilted, graduates
on a stage, but he handed them not
a degree or a decree,
not a gold, a silver, or a bronze.
Few smiled when the camera shutter closed
on their photo, on their resentment.
Some mustered manners of polite thanks.

For weeks I sorted those photos, put street
addresses to eyes and mouths staring straight
in pictures bound to become faded
manilas in musty steamer trunks.
I spent hours matching names
to gymnasts with limbs like vines,
swimmers with oxen shoulders,
equestrians with stiff spines.
Hours on full-color shots—the upshot of years
of their sweat, single-minded purpose.
I studied the faces of the sacrificed,
saw in those pictures the burden
of the strength they yielded that summer.
I also saw a good man next to them,
resolute and resourceful, knew he'd
calculated the expense, the cost-value ratio,
when he'd put those defenders
on the front line without a draft.

The Welterweight Challenge, 1980

My fingers splayed my face—that shield
of the weak-hearted—for the first-row gift
seats to the welterweight championship.
I had a little buffer when Dave Boy danced,
swung his sweat-black hair—water and salt
that seasoned men in tuxedos, women in furs.
Dave Boy hopped the stretched canvas,
sparred against Sugar Ray, swayed a fox-trot.
He hunched his shoulders into the arc of will,
whiplashed his neck back and forth
into the mitts that bobbed his eyes and nose.
His own taped and padded grips got him
out of his rural town, into the city
with the Lincoln Memorial, the White House;
but it didn't take long for Sugar Ray to flatten
him, which was good—I couldn't stomach more.
I didn't want to hear hands wrapped into stumps
thwack on jawbones or the other noises—
grunts from the ring, screams and yells
of people whose will took their bodies,
pulled them to their soles.
I didn't want to be there.
I wanted to *tell* of being there.
It was short—by round four Sugar Ray knocked
Dave Boy Green out before he hit the mat,
before he woke to the sober of a bucket of water,
before the *Post* wrote of his spirit, how he lacked
what this town wanted, this game demanded.
He was an outsider and he had fists not honed,
a head not yet punch-drunk.

The Proletariat Breakfast

It was easy to find my place in New York
at the 1980 Democratic Convention,
at offices in the Sheraton basement,
among folding tables and typewriters.
It wasn't hard to work the week
of eighteen-hour days, trudge
in the hip-sway of a cow to my room
for three hours' sleep—my days a rigor
of coffee, deli food, trips to the Garden.
It was also easy to create a tale—
an imprint—and midweek we took a lie,
made a myth, gave it a name of meaning:
the *Proletariat Breakfast*.
We all got there the same way—we just
wandered up to the cocktail parties
of trade unions, groups in the hotel,
to eat free food, imbibe in democracy
hosted by people who gather and grapple.

I joined another and then we were three:
a state coordinator, a mom-volunteer,
an assistant from Correspondence.
Soon we were a dozen going suite to suite,
campaigners who never said a private
word, had no reason to speak again.
We drifted among waiters who folded
chairs, sang *Start Spreading the News*.
We gave title to get meaning, but we
knew we weren't among the masses
nor did we look for eggs and toast.
It didn't take long before we'd made
a party into a legend, something
people *shouldn't have missed*.
But really, at dawn, in the lobby,
we'd piled into a summer-camp
pyramid—then we fell,
gathered our limbs, and went our own way.

View from the Top of a Human Pyramid on a Moving Train

The middle train-car was a frat house after finals,
a firehouse between bells, a storm cellar after furies.
For the distance from New York to D.C.
after the convention, there was reprieve.
We got beers in clouded plastic cups, pooled
like craps shooters, slouched over seats,
knelt on one knee in the aisles and sang—
Shall We Gather? Amazing Grace,
the non-apostles, Peter, Paul and Mary.
We bridged troubled water, carried heavy
brothers. We had Dan who pursed his lips
to form pure brass, (the same horn he'd play
in the unemployment line when the campaign
failed) and others on percussion, palms on chairs.

We saluted the Proletariat Breakfast, crouched
and climbed—tried to stage a pyramid on a train,
but we collapsed, became a debris of limbs
among travel bags, purses, unmatched shoes.
For a moment, we triangulated,
paused in formation, and cheers rang
beyond the cars into farms of Delaware.
I plucked a handhold of weld seams at the top
of the pyramid, curled my little finger
around grommets, jammed my knees into backs
that swayed north on a train going south.
The luggage racks became hand-grips
when the base shifted and trembled,
crumbled arm by leg by shoulder from beneath.

My view from the roof doesn't change.
Stomachs aren't paunched, the sideburns
are long, the hair's still Fawcetted.
The revelers who're gone now are still there.
At that moment we were where we wanted
to be, with the ones we wanted to be
with, doing the only thing that mattered.

We were travelers in a time contained,
and we ambled and grazed,
though without worry or need.
We had the blessings that beasts have—
we were content in the collective—
herd, flock, gaggle, campaign
moving hoof to head along graveled crossties.

The Dangers of Assuming an Outcome Because You Want It

On the first Tuesday in November, all was done.
In cities across the country, down streets
with leaves at curbs, past paint-chipped stoops,
our sound trucks cruised. They spewed and spooled
morning to night like carnival barkers.
Get Out the Vote tapes looped on eight-track
cassettes wired to speakers on pickups.

I asked Cesar Chavez to get farm workers
to vote, taped *¡A Votar!*, put it to Ray Charles'
America, America. Jesse Jackson
urged meat packers at shift change in Chicago,
and Daddy King cajoled bus drivers,
riders with swollen feet in Atlanta,
Bless you, now get out there, voters.

At the headquarters, where days, hours ago
sweat and curses rolled, there was a funeral parlor
politeness, small jokes, but I missed the meaning,
waited for the victory. And I didn't hear
the message to us, the campaigners:
Regardless of the outcome, be respectful.
I thought Ray sang about our work.

I chided the grim unslept about faith,
walked head up in delusion.
A kind man didn't try to make me listen,
rather he steered me, without a word,
into the press office, to UPI, AP wires
that spit out faint-ink Teletype. I read
the machines. They delivered concession.

The Day After Losing a Re-Election Campaign

I'd met a brash young man, ironic, not yet bitter—
and we worked days that left stomachs twisted
like wet laundry, so I said no to dinner, lunch.
Even to the note to drink a cup of coffee
at the same time, same place,
with the quarter he stuck on the page, his
thin thumb-print curled onto the scotch tape.
But the morning after the election,
when he exited his train at the moment
I exited mine, we came up the stairs together,
never said a word, just joined hands
for the walk from the K Street stop,
which, when looked at a long time later,
stands as a singular moment of worth,
when silence is enough, a full hand its own body.

Ways to Say Goodbye

They came—cabinet, senior staff—
to Andrews Air Force Base,
to send off their President, First Lady
and we watched the Capitol ceremony
of dark coats, wind-gray faces on grainy
TVs, a screen streaked even more
since we cried—all of us—until we were
worn in the weariness of defeat.
Reagan stood with his hand
on the Bible and then fifty-two
American hostages walked out of their
hold in Iran, squinted in the shock
of light, moved without the compass
needle of weaponry.
I traveled hard that afternoon
to get to regret—
plane, helicopter, bus to Plains,
to a town gathered to welcome its own.
I saw the mechanics—
the advance team sweat, the Secret Service
spin when Carter turned
and flew that night to Germany,
to greet the hostages.
And in the papers that next day—
he was the man who went to shake
the hands of gloom-eyed Americans
hunched against winter in new khakis.
He was that good man who was not
where we wanted him to be,
but there he was:
a Southern man who stood
on the tarmac to say good night,
to watch his folks go safely down the walk.

A Woman Who Knew What to Say

March, 1982. A man who once lived at the state
hospital turned to his president after Georgia
stopped locking up mental patients—he went
to the only man who could help, called
on the 17th floor of the Russell Building.
He found me instead, beseeched me, then drew
a knife that undercut words but nothing else.
If they had met, I'm not sure what either man
would have said to change things.

April, 1986. It was Mrs. Carter who stepped
to the pillow when a friend took too many pills.
President Carter stood back
in the hospital room, near the toes—
she knew how to take the young man's hand,
knew what to say to him in her quiet way.
I watched her chat—without talking about the gaps,
stigma, systemic policies, his hand on pill bottles.
She relaxed his fist, changed things.

The Outlaw at the Omni

It's an unlikely friendship—
Willie Nelson and Jimmy Carter.
One so moral, the other so Willie.
The man of Sunday School lessons,
with an ice-edge on discipline,
humbled by his leather glove
to band-saw in a garage wood shop.
And the man who shed his suit
and shorn hair in the 1950s,
who brought tension in what-to-say
tone to anyone near the two.

I looped Willie's *Unchained Melody*
around Anne Arundel County
late one night, drove that eight-track
in my Pontiac with Georgia plates
and a shot-gun campaign worker.
There was romance in the risk
of getting caught—a sign ordinance—
and while I drove, the guy jumped
out, nailed posters to poles
until a sheriff tailed,
headlamps off, inches from my trunk.

We pulled over, sat with our heads
together, lovers looking for a full moon.
We knew the law was running my
plates, was searching
for my cause, my reason.
The officer put on high beams,
screeched his tires when he drove
off without a lesson on civics,
leaving us to sail beyond ordinances,
into ordinary, into our Saturday
night messes and Sunday masses.

Willie Nelson and Jimmy Carter—
they both love a simple tune,
they've both fretted the sides of lawful.

From the stage wings of the Omni,
that first concert after Carter
left office, I watched Willie
hold up the crowd, sing
Georgia on My Mind while the people
stood with lighters towards a leader
who wrote the scores—
chords refined and chords unfinished.

When a Couple Came Late to a Wedding

At ten after twelve, my mother stood
in the narthex on the day of my wedding,
refused to walk down the aisle to her seat.
Traffic was gnarled on that Saturday—
road work stanched the ooze of traffic
and Georgia Tech played Alabama.
My guests sat in church in polite finery,
maybe making silent bets on my wedding
march, Mendelssohn or Wagner,
perhaps totaling the sum of minutes in a tie
or easing pink heels from their pinch.
An usher had already put his hand to waist,
seated the mother of the groom on the left.
My brother stood ready. Then the wedding
planner turned orchid purple when my mother
stayed the march—she saw Carter Office
staff on the church steps looking left and right.

The Carters—she didn't vote for him—were late.
His driver crackled a radio ETA in the stress
tones of a wrong turn with an annoyed passenger.
The organist peered and played, peered and played,
glanced, maybe even prayed for the waiting groom,
his hands fingering movie music to the drama
until an usher, at last, led the Carters to their seats.
Most of my guests that day forgot the sequence
of the seated, didn't notice the violinist's gout,
that a nervous groom didn't kiss the bride.
It's President Carter who always tells that story
with the chagrin of a precise man,
a man who had never been late to anything.
But he didn't know that what I saw
was a couple scurry up the church steps
with their hands joined, two who have
always moved in the hold of each other.

All of Them Mattered

A mother wrote in that gone art of cursive—
her son needed a kind word from his president.
She told how her boy was thirteen, bone cancer.
Sixty pounds of pain. He loved Jimmy Carter.
He spoke to no one and they wanted
to hear his voice in the weeks he had left.
But then his president picked up his pen
and sent him a handwritten letter so
the boy picked up his fork and began to eat.

Twenty-five years later I stood with toast
in one hand, coffee mug in the other,
paper turned to the obits. I glanced
with the contentment of the alive.
A name stored in my root-cellar of memory
was listed. A man of thirty-eight had died.
The obit told he'd been an ill child, how his
president had written to him for years—it ran
the photo of him as a man with Carter.

There were more like this story. A young
girl from Russia, a lawyer in Texas,
a miner in West Virginia, people who read
the papers and knew he was sincere,
loved his wife, was proud of his children.
A man who kept prayer lists.
They knew that after Israel and Egypt,
after interest rates and unemployment,
they could add voice to a page and be heard.

In the seventies, 220,000,000 Americans.
And 100,000 a week who wrote him.
More than one that became personal.
We were young—that ink-pot of irony—
and we found there was strength
in sentiment, that all of them mattered.
We were young when we watched a man
take words that trued when they bled into
the watermark on his azure-colored letterhead.

Later Became the Time that Stayed

I left Washington and the people who shared
the loose earth of trenches. Those,
around each other, were quiet about the task—
the way morticians never explain.
I left the workers who knew the learning
curve was an endless arc, but the good
we couldn't give the country, or give
ourselves, we gave to each other.

When I couldn't find solace in the decay
of my mother's mind, Ellen drove south
to remind an old lady she once served grits
and eggs with linen napkins. The three of us
visited in the nursing home for hours,
listened to my mother ask every ten minutes,
in a voice light as the steam on her rice,
How many children do you have?

Another time, Alicia brought the lunch, sat
without a word in the strained light
of my post-surgical afternoon.
Betty got us from the airport when I flew
home with a sick child.
And there was the time my father was ill
and Jay gave my girl
a birthday party—the one she recalls.

There were years tinted by the art of it all—
songs, stories—the time we gathered
at the Hyatt, drifted into an empty
ballroom with a piano and sang.
Or in Americus at the Best Western,
it was Tim who perfected the saga
after time warped the piqued into poignant.

There are others—Mary, Becky, Skinner.
We shared the foams and dregs of so many

beers—sweet and bitter. We don't recall
the events, only their stories—Lori, some
moment at Schwartz's Drugstore. David—
he's got a nickname that came of a handshake.
Rhonda and Scott—we've been to weddings,
births, fabled endings. People I've known young
and old, people I've known in gain and defeat.

The Family Eyes

He thought I was you, she said
as we followed the ambulance, its red,
the eyes of ill-lit Christmas pictures.
It had been a long night—the nursing home's
3:00 a.m. call: chest pains
had coursed my father from sternum to wrist.
My daughter had huddled with me
while EMTs rolled my father into a van.
I'd glared at an old fireman while I bent
over the gurney, I'd watched
him speak to my daughter—saw her
mutter, shake her head, point to me.

The fireman had seen a photo in my father's
room—me, Jimmy Carter— taken forty years
ago, after I'd worked through the night,
through November, lost sleep, humor
to dispatch Christmas cards with union bugs.
I'd been my daughter's age in that photo.
We're alike—but not just the eyes.
And we're different—she drones about drones,
she rages about Guantanamo.
She can tell you that pigs get the blues.
But she's short with me, thinks I'm made
of tatted doilies and tea cozies.

I turn the volume to Fox News down
in my head when I visit my father.
I toss NRA mail into his trash.
I don't defend folks on welfare.
But on the night the three of us drove
through the paths of streetlamps, we passed
dark houses with sleepers who snored deep
into their aloneness, dreamed in isolation.
People they loved were in those homes.
That night the three of us with the same brown
eyes sliced through the bleak and the blare.
Despite our views, I follow him, she drives me.

Simple Gifts

It was simple, really.
Thirty years later,
Vice President Mondale told
how he responded
to the ones who mocked:
We told the truth, how it was
as easy as wearing a sweater,
turning the thermostat.
We obeyed the law.
President Carter didn't twist
rule into will.
We kept the peace. No one
died in the waste of war.
That was all.
That's all that mattered
in Ferguson and Fallujah,
in the living room
or at the laundry mat.
And that was and is enough.

Acknowledgments

Thanks and heartfelt gratitude to Katie Chapel, the members of the Side Door Workshop, Ellen Hays, Jay Beck, Alicia Smith, Sevo and Dogan Eroglu, Kim Beasley, and Jud Vaughn. Love, thanks and gratitude to my daughter, Amelia Weltner, who lives in the world and words of this book, but on a different day.

About FutureCycle Press

FutureCycle Press is dedicated to publishing lasting English-language poetry books, chapbooks, and anthologies in both print-on-demand and Kindle ebook formats. Founded in 2007 by long-time independent editor/publishers and partners Diane Kistner and Robert S. King, the press incorporated as a nonprofit in 2012. A number of our editors are distinguished poets and writers in their own right, and we have been actively involved in the small press movement going back to the early seventies.

The FutureCycle Poetry Book Prize and honorarium is awarded annually for the best full-length volume of poetry we publish in a calendar year. Introduced in 2013, our Good Works projects are anthologies devoted to issues of universal significance, with all proceeds donated to a related worthy cause. Our Selected Poems series highlights contemporary poets with a substantial body of work to their credit; with this series we strive to resurrect work that has had limited distribution and is now out of print.

We are dedicated to giving all of the authors we publish the care their work deserves, making our catalog of titles the most diverse and distinguished it can be, and paying forward any earnings to fund more great books.

We've learned a few things about independent publishing over the years. We've also evolved a unique, resilient publishing model that allows us to focus mainly on vetting and preserving for posterity poetry collections of exceptional quality without becoming overwhelmed with bookkeeping and mailing, fundraising activities, or taxing editorial and production "bubbles." To find out more about what we are doing, come see us at www.futurecycle.org.

www.ingramcontent.com/pod-product-compliance
Lightning Source LLC
Chambersburg PA
CBHW070453050426
42450CB00012B/3253